Oxford Read and Discover

CW00571987

Louise Spilsbury

Contents

OXFORD

UNIVERSITY PRESS

OXFORD
UNIVERSITY PRESS

Great Clarendon Street, Oxford, OX2 6DP, United Kingdom

Oxford University Press is a department of the University of Oxford. It furthers the University's objective of excellence in research, scholarship, and education by publishing worldwide. Oxford is a registered trade mark of Oxford University Press in the UK and in certain other countries

ISBN: 978 0 19 464632 1

An Audio CD Pack containing this book and a CD is also available, ISBN 978 0 19 464642 0

The CD has a choice of American and British English recordings of the complete text.

An accompanying Activity Book is also available, ISBN 978 0 19 464653 6

Printed in China

This book is printed on paper from certified and well-managed sources.

ACKNOWLEDGEMENTS

Illustrations by: Kelly Kennedy pp.11, 15; Alan Rowe pp.21, 22, 23, 24, 25, 26, 27, 28, 30, 31

The Publishers would also like to thank the following for their kind permission to reproduce photographs and other copyright material: Alamy pp.7 (banana picking/Simon Rawles), 8 (dragon fruit/Nigel James), 10 (apples rotting/Mim Friday, avocado seedling/EuroStyle Graphics), 13 (Blickwinkel/Jagel), 15 (Foodfolio), 17; Corbis pp.3 (oranges/© AgStock Images), 4 (Ricardo Azoury), 5 (strawberry picking/Morton Beebe), 12 (monkeys/Du Huaju/Xinhua Press); Getty Images pp.3 (apples/Nick Gunderson/Stone), 7 (jackfruit/Doug Meikle Dreaming Track Images/Photolibrary), 14 (pear/Anthony Johnson/The Image Bank, lychees/Rosemary Calvert/Photographer's Choice), 16 (toast and jam/Bill Kingston/Photolibrary), 18 (Jim Jordan Photography/Taxi); Naturepl.com p.12 (bird/Dave Bevan); Oxford University Press pp.3 (bananas), 5 (passionfruit), 8 (mango), 9 (strawberries, nuts), 16 (pizza), 19; Science Photo Library p.6 (Maximilian Stock Ltd).

Introduction

All around the world there are different types of fruit. Some fruit is big and some fruit is little. Bananas, apples, and oranges are types of fruit.

Do you like to eat fruit?
What is your favorite fruit?

Now read and discover more about fruit!

Where Fruit Grows

Fruit grows on plants. Trees are a type of plant. Some types of fruit grow on big trees. Apples, oranges, peaches, and mangoes grow on big trees. Some mango trees are very tall.

Mango Trees

ground

Strawberry Plants

Kiwi Plants

Some types of fruit grow on little plants. Some fruit plants grow on the ground. Strawberry plants grow on the ground. Some fruit plants are thin, but they grow tall. Kiwi plants are tall and thin.

→ Go to page 20 for activities.

2 Different Fruit

There are many different types of fruit. Fruit can be green, red, orange, yellow, white, purple, blue, or black! Fruit can be long or short, oval or round. What shapes can you see here?

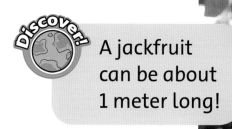

Discover!

A jackfruit can be about 1 meter long!

Different types of fruit grow in different places. Bananas and mangoes grow in hot, rainy places. Lemons and oranges grow in hot places. Apples and strawberries grow in cool places. What fruit grows where you live?

Banana Plants

→ Go to page 21 for activities.

Fruit and Seeds

All types of fruit have seeds. Some types of fruit have many little seeds. A dragon fruit has many little seeds.

Some types of fruit have one big seed. A mango has one big seed. Open some fruit to see the seeds inside!

Dragon Fruit

many little seeds

Mangoes

one big seed

seed

Discover! A strawberry has seeds on the outside!

Some types of fruit are soft. Oranges, strawberries, and peaches are soft.

Some types of fruit are hard. Nuts are hard. Nuts have seeds inside.

Inside a Nut

seed

→ Go to page 22 for activities.

 # New Fruit Plants

What do seeds do? Seeds make new plants! Old fruit falls from a plant to the ground. The fruit rots. The seeds from the fruit go into the ground. New plants grow from the seeds.

Old Fruit

A New Plant

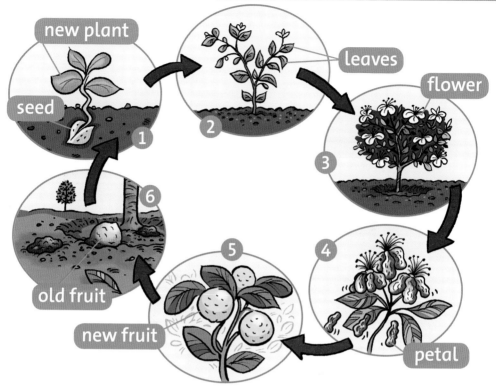

① A seed in the fruit makes a new plant.

② Leaves make food for the new plant so it can grow.

③ Flowers grow on the plant.

④ The flowers get old and the petals fall from the plant.

⑤ New fruit grows.

⑥ Old fruit falls to the ground and rots.

→ Go to page 23 for activities.

5 Fruit and Animals

A Bird

Many animals eat fruit. Birds, monkeys, and mice eat fruit. They eat it in the trees and on the ground.

Many animals eat little fruit seeds. Animals don't eat very big fruit seeds.

Monkeys

Some animals carry fruit to a new place. Then they eat it. They drop fruit seeds on the ground. New plants grow from the seeds. It's good for plants to grow in a new place. They can grow big and tall.

A Plant in a New Place

Go to page 24 for activities. 13

How to Eat Fruit

flesh

skin

seed

A Pear

Open a fruit and look inside! Can you see the skin, flesh, and seeds?

A Lychee

Some fruit skin isn't good to eat. We peel the skin. Then we eat the flesh inside. We can do this with lychees, mangoes, and bananas.

Some fruit skin is good to eat. We wash the fruit skin with cold water. Then we eat the skin and flesh. We can do this with apples, peaches, and grapes.

We can use the skin of the mangosteen fruit to make medicine!

→ Go to page 25 for activities.

Jam

We use soft fruit to make jam. We use fruit to make cakes and cookies, too.

olive oil

pizza

Olives and tomatoes are types of fruit. We use tomatoes to make pizza. We press olives to make olive oil. We use olive oil to cook food.

Fruit Juice

We press some fruit to make fruit juice. Do you like to drink orange, apple, or pineapple juice?

We mix some fruit with milk or ice cream to make milkshakes.

→ Go to page 26 for activities.

8 It's Good for You!

Fruit is good for your heart, eyes, and skin. Fruit is good for your body. It can stop you getting sick. Fruit helps you to walk, run, play, learn, and grow.

You can eat fruit when you are hungry. You can eat fruit when you are thirsty, too. Fruit has water inside. It stops you being thirsty!

It's good to eat two or three different types of fruit every day. Fruit is good for you!

→ Go to page 27 for activities.

① Where Fruit Grows

← Read pages 4–5.

1 Complete the sentences

| mango   Trees   fruit   ~~plants~~   grow |

1 Fruit grows on ___plants___ .

2 _____ are a type of plant.

3 Some types of _____ grow on big trees.

4 Oranges _____ on big trees.

5 Some _____ trees are very tall.

2 Match.

1 Apples grow

2 Some types of fruit grow on

3 Some fruit plants grow

4 Strawberry plants

5 Kiwi plants

grow on the ground.

are tall and thin.

little plants.

on big trees.

on the ground.

2 Different Fruit

← Read pages 6–7.

apple   strawberry
orange   lemon
~~banana~~   mango

1 Write the words.

1 _banana_
2 _____
3 _____
4 _____
5 _____
6 _____

2 Complete the sentences

grow   cool   rainy   cool   places   hot

1 Mangoes grow in hot, rainy _____ .

2 Bananas grow in hot, _____ places.

3 Lemons grow in _____ places.

4 Apples grow in _____ places.

5 Oranges _____ in hot places.

6 Strawberries grow in _____ places.

3 Fruit and Seeds

← Read pages 8–9.

1 Write the words.

> soft fruit   one big seed
> hard fruit   many little seeds

1 _____   3 _____

2 _____   4 _____

2 Write *true* or *false*.

1 All types of fruit have seeds.   _true_

2 Some types of fruit have
many little seeds.   _____

3 Some types of fruit have one big seed. _____

4 Oranges and peaches are hard.   _____

5 Nuts are soft.   _____

④ New Fruit Plants

← Read pages 10–11.

1 Write the numbers.

- [ ] Petals fall from the plant.
- [ ] Flowers grow on the plant.
- [ ] Leaves make food for the new plant so it can grow.
- [ ] Old fruit falls to the ground and rots.
- [ ] New fruit grows.
- [1] A seed in the fruit makes a new plant.

2 Find and write the words.

flowerspetalsseedsplantsgroundleaves

1 __flowers__   3 _____   5 _____

2 _____   4 _____   6 _____

5 Fruit and Animals

← Read pages 12–13.

1 Complete the puzzle.

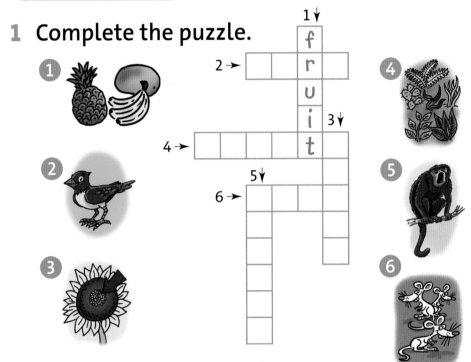

2 Circle the correct words.

1 Some animals carry fruit to a (new) / old place.

2 Some animals drop fruit seeds on the ground / grow.

3 New **plants** / **places** grow from the seeds.

4 It's good for plants to **grow** / **eat** in a new place.

6 How to Eat Fruit

← Read pages 14–15.

1 **Write the words.**   flesh   skin   seeds

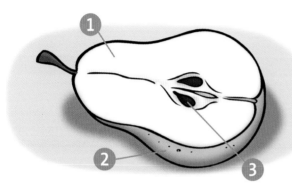

1 _____

2 _____

3 _____

2 **Complete the sentences.**

fruit   skin   skin   flesh   peel   wash

1 We _____ the skin from lychees,
   mangoes, and bananas. Then we eat the
   _____ inside.

2 We _____ fruit skin with cold water.
   Then we eat the _____ and the flesh.

3 We can use the _____ of the
   mangosteen _____ to make medicine.

7 Food and Drink

← Read pages 16–17.

1 Write the words.

> jam   olive oil   juice   pizza

1 _____   3 _____

2 _____   4 _____

2 Match.

1 We press fruit
2 We use soft fruit to
3 We use tomatoes
4 We press olives
5 We use olive oil

to make olive oil.
to make pizza.
make jam.
to cook food.
to make fruit juice.

(8) It's Good for You!

← Read pages 18–19.

1 Circle the correct words.

1 (eyes) / heart   2 body / skin

3 learn / walk   4 run / play   5 grow / eat

2 Write *true* or *false*.

1 Fruit is good for your body.   _____

2 Fruit can stop you getting sick.   _____

3 Fruit helps you to learn and grow.   _____

4 Fruit has no water inside.   _____

5 Fruit makes you thirsty.   _____

6 It's good to eat fruit every day.   _____

Fruit

1 Draw and write the fruit that you eat in a week.

Monday		I banana I apple I fruit juice

Day	Draw	Write
Monday		
Tuesday		
Wednesday		
Thursday		
Friday		
Saturday		
Sunday		

2 Complete the sentences about fruit.

There are many different _____ _____

Fruit stops you _____ _____

Eat two or three _____ _____

Fruit

Fruit grows on _____ _____

All fruit has _____ _____

Seeds make _____ _____

Fruit is good _____ _____

Picture Dictionary

cook

cool

drop

fall

flesh

grapes

ground

grow

hard

inside

jam

leaves

lychees

mangoes

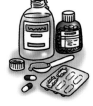
medicine

melons

 mice

 mix

 olives

 olive oil

 peaches

 peel

 petals

 plants

 press

 rot

 seeds

 shapes

 skin

 soft

 strawberries

 world

Oxford Read and Discover

Series Editor: Hazel Geatches • CLIL Adviser: John Clegg

Oxford Read and Discover graded readers are at six levels, for students from age 6 and older. They cover many topics within three subject areas, and support English across the curriculum, or Content and Language Integrated Learning (CLIL).

Available for each reader:
- Audio CD Pack (book & audio CD)
- Activity Book

Teaching notes & CLIL guidance: **www.oup.com/elt/teacher/readanddiscover**

Subject Area / Level	The World of Science & Technology	The Natural World	The World of Arts & Social Studies
1 300 headwords	• Eyes • Fruit • Trees • Wheels	• At the Beach • In the Sky • Wild Cats • Young Animals	• Art • Schools
2 450 headwords	• Electricity • Plastic • Sunny and Rainy • Your Body	• Camouflage • Earth • Farms • In the Mountains	• Cities • Jobs
3 600 headwords	• How We Make Products • Sound and Music • Super Structures • Your Five Senses	• Amazing Minibeasts • Animals in the Air • Life in Rainforests • Wonderful Water	• Festivals Around the World • Free Time Around the World
4 750 headwords	• All About Plants • How to Stay Healthy • Machines Then and Now • Why We Recycle	• All About Desert Life • All About Ocean Life • Animals at Night • Incredible Earth	• Animals in Art • Wonders of the Past
5 900 headwords	• Materials to Products • Medicine Then and Now • Transportation Then and Now • Wild Weather	• All About Islands • Animal Life Cycles • Exploring Our World • Great Migrations	• Homes Around the World • Our World in Art
6 1,050 headwords	• Cells and Microbes • Clothes Then and Now • Incredible Energy • Your Amazing Body	• All About Space • Caring for Our Planet • Earth Then and Now • Wonderful Ecosystems	• Food Around the World • Helping Around the World